THE EXCITEMENT OF TEACHING

KAPPA DELTA PI LECTURE SERIES

WITH The Excitement of Teaching as the third volume the Kappa Delta Pi Lectureship Series continues the discussion of the broader and cultural phases of Education as interpreted by distinguished scholars whose educational interests are professional and general. In the present volume Professor Phelps, long an eminent teacher, views his profession not as a drudgery but as an exciting adventure among young lives. With literature as a background he indicates and illustrates that teaching is essentially an art, and that its supreme outcome is an individual equipped to engage in the fine art of living and in the art of fine living.

THE EXCITEMENT OF TEACHING

BY WILLIAM LYON PHELPS

FORMERLY INSTRUCTOR IN HISTORY AND LITERATURE AT WESTMIN-
STER SCHOOL. FORMERLY MORGAN FELLOW AND INSTRUCTOR
IN ENGLISH AT HARVARD. LAMPSON PROFESSOR OF
ENGLISH LITERATURE AT YALE

LIVERIGHT PUBLISHING CORP.

NEW YORK

PREFACE

THIS little book is a revision and an enlargement of an address given on 24 February 1931 in Detroit, at a public meeting called by Kappa Delta Pi, a national educational society. I wish to express here my grateful appreciation of the honour of the invitation.

W. L. P.

Yale University
Tuesday 11 August 1931

TABLE OF CONTENTS

[I]

LITERATURE AS A REVELATION OF LIFE

IN a novel published in 1930, *Green Isle*, by Alice Duer Miller, I found the story and the characters interesting, but the following paragraph more interesting than either:

Strangely enough there is nowhere the average person can go to learn how to live his daily life. Children are taught Latin and astronomy, but no school or college tells them how to clear their mind for a decision, how to tell certain psychological, or even psychopathic types, and how to deal with them; how, for any individual, to draw the line between idleness and serenity, between overwork and fullness of life, between sweet charity and being every man's dupe. Everybody needs such instruction, something halfway between religious precepts and practical talks to salesmen. Women need it particularly, for they do not get, as early as men do, the experience of the business world.

9

It is quite true, that even among the prodigious number of things professionally taught in some universities today, like cream-separating, nursing, scene-painting, advertising, fertilising, short-story writing, and among the increasing number of "business colleges," "schools of journalism," "schools of the drama," there are no graduate schools devoted to the art of living, and no professional teachers employed to specialise in Life. Possibly the nearest approach to it is the professorship of "evil" held by a wise woman, Corra Harris, in that interesting academic experiment, Rollins College in Florida.

Yet the paradox is that the less practical, the less "efficient" the particular subject and the particular method of teaching may be, the more the average person will learn how to live his daily life. In a course on electrical engineering, taught by a first-class teacher to a picked class of superior pupils, there will probably be little knowledge gleaned on how to prepare one's mind for a decision, and how to distinguish between sweet charity and being every man's dupe. But in a course in Greek literature, the students may learn little if their proficiency is determined by the ease with which they can read Greek at sight; but they cannot help learning something —and some of them will learn much—about the art of living.

It is curious that many people believe in the importance of what they call vocational and practical courses, and regard the study of great literature as merely ornamental, a pretty accomplishment all well enough in seminaries for young ladies. As a matter of fact, nothing is more essential in the proper furnishing of a man's mind than a knowledge of the world's best literature—poetry, fiction, essays, drama. Literature is the immortal part of history. Literature is the interpretation of human life.

It is unfortunate that the majority of pupils in high schools and colleges do not study literature with the concentrated attention they give later to vocational and professional studies. They do not see the connexion between "liberal" studies and success in life, but they ought to.

I asked a successful engineer in Boston, a man who is at the head of enterprises where he has scores of young engineers working under him, this question: "What studies in college would you advise for one who intends to become a civil engineer?" He replied without any hesitation, "Anything so long as it has no connexion with engineering." He told me that those who came to him from technical schools with no liberal education began at first to surpass those who had studied literature and other general subjects. But in a few years the truly "educated" young men went ahead, because they had imagination, interesting minds, and a knowledge of human nature.

I should not urge boys and girls to read good books because it will make them successful lawyers, physicians, engineers, business men; it is better to be a good father, a good husband, a good son, a good brother, a good friend, than to achieve material success; it is better to be an interesting personality than to be an efficient machine. But just as a physician who has an admirable "bedside manner" is more successful than one who carries an atmosphere of chill, so it is certain that a knowledge of human nature, with the sympathy, tolerance, and understanding that should accompany such knowledge, is an asset for success in any calling where one comes into contact with people.

One reason why Greek and Roman literature makes an unexcelled foundation for modern problems is, that it forms a *closed subject.* Nothing can be taken away from it, nothing can be added to it. Modern science is shifting its ground every day; an astronomer will tell you that if you want to keep up with astronomy, you must read the newspapers. The fundamental propositions of Economics, the foundations of the whole structure, are being challenged; and the reputation of modern authors shifts in value like stocks in Wall Street. But the dramatists, poets, philosophers, statesmen, warriors of Greece and Rome are fixed and unchangeable. The outward circumstances of their lives were certainly different from ours; they did not live in an age of machines; but their desires and dislikes, their pleasures and pains, their ambitions and sensations were the same as ours, because *human nature has never changed.*

In order to study any form of life under the microscope, the observer must isolate it; and in some respects it is easier to study human nature in the literature of that period than in our own, because the circumstances of living were simple. George Moore told me that in his next novel he was going back to the ancient Greeks, because in our day the automobile, the radio, etc., etc., had overlaid human nature with such a cloud of complexities that it was difficult to see naked emotions in their natural sincerity.

As there is nothing more interesting than human nature, and no better revelation of human nature than is found in good litera-ture, so the teaching of literature is or should be exciting for both teacher and pupil. They see together the long, unfolding drama of humanity with its almost infinite variety of individual

13

manifestations, and yet with its fundamental qualities unchanged and unchangeable.

Carl Schurz, who played so prominent a part in American political history, paid the following tribute to the educational value of the ancient classics:

They lead us irrisistibly to an ideal view of men and things. In the literature of antiquity, man is magnified beyond his natural dimensions. We see him mostly divested of the common cares of life and occupied with great things only, whether absorbed in meditative contemplation or active in the great affairs of State. The misty distance which separates us from him like an airy vision lends grandeur to all his motions and attitudes; and this spectacle of human life on the grandest scale transports us above the common level of everyday sentiments.—This is not all. Classical literature excels all other in the harmonious chastity of form. In a democratic organization of society like ours, we become apt to forget what influence the beauty of form exercises upon the mind. It imparts to us a sensitiveness of feeling which often, almost imperceptibly, determines the current of our thoughts.... In my opinion, the stronger we lean to the side of the material, the more it is necessary that we should promote, by education, the culture of the ideal. In cultivating the noble and beautiful along with the useful, we should evade that onesidedness of character which may make a people for a while rich but not good, powerful but not great. (From *The Americanization of Carl Schurz* by Chester Verne Easum.)

14

Whether one sets out on a voyage to Europe or on a voyage through life, it is fortunate if one can have something fixed and eternal, something on which one may confidently rely. It is a fortunate thing for navigation in the night that the needle of the compass points toward the North; and it is fortunate for one having to make his way through the darker and more devious courses in life, that human nature is invariable. A treatise on chemistry published in 1904 is as useless as the almanac of that year; whereas *Hamlet* published in 1604, and a play by Euripides, produced in 406 B.C., are as true for 1931 as they were for their own age and generation.

Gladstone, the champion in Parliamentary debate, was the leading authority of his time on intricate questions of public finance: his preparation was based on Homer and Horace: Lord Morley, who had to deal with perplexing problems in Ireland and India, was a profound student of the classics: I heard Lord Chief Justice Coleridge say in his old age, that he had read something either in Greek or Latin every day of his professional life: Lord Arthur Balfour was familiar both with the classics and with the wise books of the East.

It is a curious thing that we call novels "works of fiction" when they are works of eternal truth.

The reason for the continued popularity of Charles Dickens—every year more copies of his books are sold than those by any recent writer—is, that he gave us faithful portraits of the virtues and vices, the hypocrisies and follies, the strength and the weakness of human nature. If every minister of the gospel would attentively study the characters Chadband and Stiggins, he would learn, anyhow, what not to do. He would learn to drop the insufferable "holy tone" which many ministers use in reading the Bible and in preaching; he would learn not to state self-evident commonplaces as though they were revelations; he would learn never to say anything that he did not himself believe. Insincerity is a sure road to failure.

Every man and woman who reads Dickens attentively would learn not to treat children either with disdain or with condescension. When a speaker addressing a school begins by saying "How sweet it is today to look into your bright, eager young faces" he ought to know that every child in the room suffers from nausea; and he would know it, if he had read Dickens. Perhaps the highest test of a gentleman is his treatment of children. Observe in Dickens the number of times a man begins his approach to a boy by ruffling his hair. "Well, my little man, and how is the world treating you?" Dickens has given us again and again the fierce resentment of children when they are treated by their elders either with indifference or with an insinuating grin.

One of the worst afflictions is the Bore. The Bore is one who insists on talking only on the theme that interests him, and usually at the most inopportune moment. Dickens has given us many portraits of bores, and if we are wise, we shall profit by observing them. The Bore is often a more devastating curse than the professional criminal.

In reading the Russian novels of the three masters, Turgenev, Tolstoi, and Dostoevski, we find there is in reality no such thing as a separate "Russian Soul." There are only human souls in Russia. Tolstoi was one hundred per cent Russian. He came of a long line of Russian ancestry, and although he spoke many languages, he wrote only in Russian. Yet he had more influence on the world than any other man of his time, because whether he wrote a historical novel like *War and Peace* or a contemporary novel like *Anna Karenina,* he was so faithful to the facts of human nature that every one felt the impact of recognition. Sometimes when a friend shows us an oil portrait of himself and hopes we shall like it, we see instantly that it is not a good likeness, and then, in order not to hurt his feelings, we take refuge in common-place phrases. But the moment Tolstoi gives us a portrait of a man or a woman, we recognise its likeness. There is in human nature no caprice so trivial, no passion so terrible, as to be beyond the skill of this Russian genius.

When Turgenev said that for every age love has its tortures and then illustrated it by human examples, he said something that, if we are wise, and able to profit by what we learn, we may be saved from the valley of humiliation. When Browning, in that masterpiece of passion, *In a Balcony*, showed that it was quite possible for a woman of fifty to fall terribly in love with a young man, he not only gave us an accurate picture of the human heart, but also a plain danger signal.

After all, the best lessons are those we learn for ourselves by contemplation of the truth. Direct teaching, eloquent exhortation, are not so impressive as accurate representations, wherein we may see the way of life and the way of death. The teacher need simply make the contact between the student and the masterpiece.

For success in politics, the maxims of the ancient Chinese philosopher Confucius are as applicable this moment in Nebraska and in New Jersey as they were when first uttered in China.

A mind well-stored with wisdom of the East has a mint of current coin.

The great truth that no one can really be injured except by himself was well known to the ancient Greeks. By such a statement is meant, of course, that the integrity of one's mind, one's personality, can be injured only by oneself. Powerful human enemies, bad weather, ill-health, and the various misfortunes that flesh is heir to can hurt one bodily and can reduce one's physical and financial assets. But the inner life of a man is secure against all outside attack, and can be injured or destroyed only by himself. Aeschylus expressed this idea in a fine figure of speech:

> So in the Libyan fable it is told
> That once an eagle, stricken with a dart,
> Said, when he saw the fashion of the shaft,
> "With our own feathers, not by others' hands,
> Are we now smitten."

The fact that human nature, the main subject of study by great dramatists, poets, and novelists, has always been so interesting that anything that concerns humanity, no matter how trivial, is worth thinking about, was stated once for all by Terence, who lived in the second century before Christ: "I am a man, and nothing that concerns a man is a matter of indifference to me." Again Terence said: "I bid him look into the lives of others as in a mirror, and from others to take an example for himself."

Many people today lament the fact that family discipline is weak; that instead of the father of the family controlling his children, telling them where they shall go, what they shall read, it is the other way around. The child rules the house; the whole family humbly obey his caprices. Today, when a play of questionable taste is being discussed, the daughter describes it by saying, "Well, it is not exactly the kind of piece I should take mother to see." This situation is not so new as many imagine. Plutarch says that one day, Themistocles, laughing at his own son, who got his mother, and by his mother's means his father also, to indulge him, told him that he had the most power of any one in Greece: "the Athenians command the rest of Greece, I command the Athenians, your mother commands me, and you command your mother."

Everything seems to have been said; all we can hope to do is to express old truths and old ideas in a fresh way. Even most jokes are old; if any one imagines the step-mother has only recently become an object of satire, let me call his attention to Plutarch, who said that once upon a time a man threw a stone at a bitch, and hit his step-mother, on which he said, "Not so bad!"

20

Nearly everybody imagines he is worse off than others; that he has particularly bad luck; that he never had a fair chance; or in other words, the majority of mankind suffers from the insidious poison of self-pity. Consider what Socrates said on this question: that if all human misfortunes were placed in one common heap, and everyone told he must take an equal portion with others, most people would be glad to take their own and depart.

One of the chief reasons for success in life is the ability to maintain a daily interest in one's work, to have a *chronic* enthusiasm; to regard each day as important. This was seen and expressed by Marcus Aurelius, when he said, "In the morning, when thou art sluggish at rousing thee, let this thought be present: I am rising to a man's work." He also defined happiness as doing the things that are proper to a man.

If one really wishes to be superior in mind and character to the common herd, one must follow the ideals one has set for oneself and not follow those of the mass. It will not do for him to say he is no worse than others; that he lives as others do; that he pays his enemies in their own coin. He must have standards that are his, and that are in no respect determined by what others do. If, in playing golf, his opponent hands in a false score, he should not try to even matters by playing false himself; he must stick to his own ideals and methods, regardless of what his neighbors, competitors, or antagonists do. This splendid way of living was never better expressed than by the foremost statesman of antiquity, Julius Cæsar. It is well to be acquainted with the letters that passed between him and Cicero, because the interchange of noble minds is profitable and inspiring. Julius Cæsar had just pardoned his most bitter and dangerous enemies, and set them free, regardless of what they might do. Cicero approved of this and wrote to tell him so; but Cicero also expressed the fear that these villains might use their new freedom to take arms once more against Cæsar; to which letter Cæsar replied in these magnanimous words: "I rejoice that my action in pardoning my enemies meets with your approval. Nor do I care if those whom I have pardoned once more take up arms against me; for it is my glory to live according to my own ideals and let my enemies live according to theirs."

In teaching a group of young men or young women today, it is easy to see how such a remark as Cæsar's lends excitement to the study of ancient history. If we are looking for ideals in sportsmanship, we can find the highest in this standard set by the greatest mind of Rome.

Not only do we get common sense and the art of practical living from great literature, no matter in what country or in what period of time it was written, we learn something more than the rules of business, we obtain inspiration for hours of despondency or danger. I do not know why it is that the men who have gone toward the South Pole have excelled in character and grace and charm those who have been identified with the North; but consider four splendid names —Amundsen, Scott, Shackleton, Byrd. When Shackleton and his men were caught in the ice, and there appeared only a very small chance of escape, and that chance depended entirely on being able to walk many miles, the gallant leader addressed his men. He told them to throw away every weight, as any unnecessary thing might destroy their lives. They threw away extra clothing, though the weather was terrible; they threw away some food, though they were hungry; then Shackleton, with his men looking on, drew from his pockets many gold sovereigns, and dropped them one by one through a crevice in the ice, and they went to the bottom of the Antarctic Sea. After these notable sacrifices, he exhibited a copy of the poems of Robert Browning, and said that on no account would he throw away this book. These poems, during the nights in the ice-huts, he would read

23

aloud to the company, and he believed their value would be greater in inspiration than their weight in money, food, or clothes. Nothing more need be said on the actual value of an acquaintance with great literature.

One day in Berlin I was talking with the famous German dramatist, Gerhart Hauptmann. I asked him if his plays expressed his own opinions. "No," said he, "they do not always express my own opinions; but any intelligent reader of five or six of my dramas ought to know the kind of man I am." So, in reading Shakespeare, we learn that the thing he admired most in men was self-control, moderation; he hated excess, and despised those who never could control their instincts and passions. When Hamlet told Horatio that he valued his friend above all others because he was not "passion's slave," he pointed out to his readers a safe path through the perils of life.

The Authorised version of the Bible is the greatest of all works of literature; for it is the best translation of the best book in the world. This translation was made in the most splendid creative period; it was made and completed during the life of Shakespeare. From the purely literary point of view, English-speaking people have a better Bible than the French or the Germans or the Italians or the Spanish; the translation is even better than the original Hebrew and Greek. This incomparably rich inheritance is free to all who can read English.

I do not know of a single distinguished writer of English verse or prose during the last three hundred years who does not show in his work familiarity with the Bible. Some authors, like Bunyan, founded their style on it; some poems, like Kipling's *Recessional,* are purely Biblical. Great orators like Gladstone and Daniel Webster were saturated in the Bible; to any young man or woman today, who has ambition to write —and who has not?—my first advice would be, *Read the Bible.*

Professor John A. Scott, professor of Greek in Northwestern University, says:

In understanding and interpreting Luke I have but one advantage over the person who knows no Greek, and that is this: My knowledge of Greek gives me an elevation from which I can better appreciate the towering worth, beauty, and accuracy of the King James version. Anyone who can read this version has everything at his command. Professor Gildersleeve, who made Johns Hopkins University famous, and is by common consent the greatest Greek scholar whom America has produced, after comparing the King James version with all the various versions appearing before 1920, pronounced the King James version on the side of Greek the greatest accomplishment of the English-speaking race.

The Bible itself, either in the original or in any language, is the single greatest inspiration to modern literature. Tolstoi, the foremost man of letters since Goethe; Dostoevski, Turgenev, Chekhov all knew the Bible. Herzen, the great Russian revolutionist and literary critic, could not read the Gospels without tears.

Ibsen, in speaking of various authors that had helped him, said "My chief source of inspiration is the Bible; it is strong and mighty." But it is needless to multiply illustrations; the Bible is the foundation not only of the best civilisation but of the best literature.

And we get from the Bible not only religious elevation and moral guidance; we learn tact, good manners, unselfish consideration. These qualities contain the secret of genuine popularity.

For whatever may be thought nowadays of the historical and scientific accuracy of the Bible, whatever we may think of the historicity of the Garden of Eden and of the animals in the Ark, there is surely one portion of the Bible that is just as definitely and accurately true today as when it was first written. That is the Book of Proverbs, the accumulated wisdom of experience.

[II]

FIVE PILLARS OF EDUCATION

I SHALL always remember a conversation I had some twenty years ago with a cultivated Englishman, Mr. E. Nelson Fell. He attended one of the most famous preparatory schools in the world, Eton. Now these preparatory schools are so-called because they prepare one for the university; but Mr. Fell did not proceed to the university. He found that Eton prepared him for life. He became a business man, and was sent into a remote part of Russia, where as Superintendent of a vast enterprise, he had under his direction several hundred Russian peasants, *muzhiks*. His educational preparation for this undertaking consisted of the Greek, Latin, Mathematics he had been forced to study at school.

He not only was obliged to have a thorough

knowledge of the immense construction work on which he was engaged; he had to manage these peasants, who had adult bodies and infantile minds. Every day he had to make sudden and important decisions; every day he had to draw the line between charity and imposition; every day he had to diagnose and diagnose correctly certain psychological and even psychopathic types. His efforts were crowned with success; the enterprise was profitable from the financial point of view, and the peasants, despite occasional outbreaks, were devoted to him heart and soul. He told me that he regarded his years at Eton as the most valuable training he could possibly have had for this particular task. He thought it more valuable than any special training in business management, the psychology of labour, or "personality."

Apparently he learned at Eton something that was not part of the curriculum—he learned the very things that Mrs. Miller says no school or college imparts. How did this happen? In order to find out, I will refer those who are interested to a recent book by an experienced English principal, Doctor Cyril Norwood, who has summarised the wisdom acquired in many years of teaching in a book called *The English Tradition of Education.*

Doctor Norwood, Headmaster of Harrow,

declares there are five foundations of school education. These are Religion, Discipline, Culture, Athletics, Public Service.

So far as I know, Mr. Fell never came into contact with Doctor Norwood; but his specific experiences seem to be excellent illustrations of Doctor Norwood's five abstract principles.

Doctor Norwood believes thoroughly in compulsory daily religious services in preparatory schools. He is fully aware of the serious objections to the scheme, and the difficulties that stand in the way of its operation; but he is sure the advantages outweigh the drawbacks. He knows that many boys find the service anything but religious; they are not in a pious mood when they enter the chapel, they are not pious during the service, they are not pious when they leave. Many of the teachers who conduct chapel are perfunctory, mechanical, uninspiring; many of the visiting preachers who fill the pulpit on Sundays are tiresome and sometimes ridiculous.

Mr. Fell said that when he was at Eton he often felt in a rebellious mood about "compulsory religion" and so did many of the other boys; if they had had their way, they would have abolished daily and Sunday chapel. But looking back on it in later life, he believed it had been immensely beneficial; there were days when a sermon was preached that had a powerful and

29

lasting effect; there were weekday mornings, when entering chapel in anything but a religious mood, some magnificent phrase from the Bible had arrested his attention. Furthermore, religion was *there,* it was there every day; they were constantly exposed to it; seeds were planted in their minds of which they were at the time unconscious, but which later came to fruition. For religion is the greatest adventure of the human spirit; and any great adventure is exciting.

And with all the evident objections, what is the alternative to compulsory chapel? The alternative is that the majority of the boys would go through the whole course at Eton without once being brought into contact with religion—that is to say, with one of the foundations of Anglo-Saxon civilisation. This is the condition of affairs today in many American universities.

Thus in this matter the principles of Doctor Norwood were supported by the experience of Mr. Fell.

The second foundation, Discipline, has today an unpleasant odour. But was there ever a time when discipline was more needed? A disciplined mind with a disciplined body is a good combination. Doctor Norwood has little sympathy with the modern democratic idea that discipline should be in the hands of the pupils; that it should come from below up, instead of from the authorities down. He does not believe that schoolboys should decide what they shall study, or when they shall study, or where they shall study. He believes that the very students who find discipline most irksome are the ones who in late life will be most insistent on its enforcement, especially where their own children are concerned. He believes also that where the necessity for discipline is properly explained to the students, and enforced reasonably, most of them will realise its necessity; and others can go to some other school, where they will not be annoyed.

Well, in stating the reasons why he found the course at Eton so valuable in the management of a Russian factory, Mr. Fell laid especial emphasis on the rigid discipline. He had been taught not only that he must perform certain tasks, whether palatable or not, but that he must perform them at a certain time. This is exactly the situation that confronts most men in the life of the world, and he had been trained not only to meet special emergencies, but to do the daily routine work as thoroughly and cheerfully as possible.

I think American universities today, in their laudable desire to have students "take the initiative," to feel their own responsibility for work, instead of having instruction ladled out to them by the spoonful, are in grave danger of losing something that can positively be attained in order to accomplish something that may not be accomplished at all. It is quite true that no teacher can force a pupil to master a given subject; that no teacher can force a pupil to do original thinking. But any teacher can force any pupil, on peril of dismissal, to attend recitations and lectures at assigned hours; to hand in written work at an assigned moment; in other words, to keep his engagements. This kind of discipline can really—and not necessarily disagreeably—be enforced, and it is certainly part of one's preparation for the art of living. But where the student is left to himself to decide whether or not he will attend classes, whether or not he will have his work done at a given time, whether or not he will work at all, the danger is or ought to be obvious. I remember once, a good many years ago, the students at a certain college were informed that they were all gentlemen, not prisoners, and would be treated as such. Thus they were to decide for themselves whether it was to their advantage to attend "routine" lectures, or whether they could do better work in their rooms or at the college library. In the month of February a man from Chicago came on to see his son, who was an undergraduate; he found the boy was cruising in the Caribbean Sea. The college authorities had some difficulty in defending themselves against the charge of taking money on false pretences.

Of course I am not arguing that university instruction should resemble in its methods the manner of the primary school. Students who in the first two years of college have proved their ability and their love of learning, may then profitably enjoy certain privileges of independence. Every man of genius in literature or in painting or in music who shows independence by breaking the rules, has first learned what those rules are.

By culture Doctor Norwood means actual and accurate knowledge of something, not a smattering, not even a society accomplishment. Profound culture often produces a high excitement. I have read books of literary criticism that are truly exciting. Just as it was exciting for adventurers in the Klondike to find gold, so it is exciting for students to discover the riches of literature. Was there ever a better illustration of the excitement of learning than Keats's description of how he felt when he discovered the riches of Homer, revealed to him by Chapman? His testimony has the significant title, *On First*

Looking Into Chapman's Homer. How did he *feel?*

> Then felt I like some watcher of the skies
> When a new planet swims into his ken.

Some of the happiest moments in my career as a professional teacher have come from the excitement in the minds of young men when the previously hidden treasure of some great poet comes into their possession.

We all know what is meant in literary scholarship by the phrase "enthusiasm of discovery." It is a form of excitement. . . .

Very few subjects were taught at Eton; in comparison with the alluring programme of attractive "up to date" practical things spread out over a wide area and spread out thin at other institutions, the Eton curriculum seemed singularly narrow. But the boys got a sound knowledge of the history and social conditions of the ancient world; and as human nature has never changed, they found that knowledge applicable to most modern conditions.

Here again Mr. Fell declared that not only the training he got in the study of the Greek and Latin languages, but the actual knowledge he acquired of Greek and Latin culture, were of enormous value to him in his job of managing

34

not only a Russian factory, but Russian work-men.

Athletics form one of the foundations of English school life, and when kept within reasonable limits, one of the best means of training for the subsequent career. The development of muscle is perhaps the least of the desirable results attained, though important enough in itself. Courage is the foundation of all the virtues; unless a man has that virtue, said Doctor Johnson, he has no security for preserving any other. Athletics develop courage; they develop resource in the face of an emergency; they develop good sportsmanship, which consists in playing every game fairly, in respect and consideration for an opponent, in ability to take victory without conceit and defeat without excuse. They develop qualities of leadership, and qualities of obedience. For however evil may be the smell of discipline in intellectual, moral, and religious affairs, the absolute enforcement of strict discipline with immediate and unquestioning obedience to authority, is taken for granted in matters like football. But the discipline could not be enforced unless both the subject taught and the method of coaching were exciting.

The danger in athletics is not the danger in studies. There is no danger that most boys or girls will study too much or give undue importance to the training of the mind or to the acquirement of knowledge. But there is danger always and everywhere that athletic sports will take a disproportionate place in the student's mind.

Outside of schools and colleges, a vast number of newspaper readers demand to know which is the best team in the country; who is national champion? What players should be selected as All-American? This leads to sectional championships, and by the process of elimination, which requires railway travel of thousands of miles, and corresponding absence from college, to the national championship; and very soon we shall not be content with that, but must discover by the same process, what institution of learning is the World Athletic Champion.

University undergraduates are as a rule modest, sensible, reasonable, and gifted with humour; their pictures and biographies on the sporting pages of newspapers are not taken with undue seriousness. A leading athlete, at this moment an undergraduate at Harvard, Barry Wood, who has attained distinction in three major sports and who is also a member of Phi Beta Kappa, has too much sense and too much intelligence to be upset by printed praise. But how about boys of fifteen and sixteen, in High Schools and Preparatory Schools, who see in the newspapers enormous pictures of themselves in action, with long and detailed biographies?

Here again, Mr. Fell, while not an athlete, got at Eton enough training in body and character through athletic sports, to be of much assistance to him in his daily struggle with difficult conditions in Russia.

The fifth foundation of education, according to Doctor Norwood, is public service, in one word, unselfishness. Here he is an optimist, as I think every modern teacher must be. Whatever we may think of the decline of Protestant church-going (there is no indication of such a thing among the Catholics), whatever we may think of the decline of intellectual discipline or of the decline of sound culture, or of the excess of interest in athletics, there is not the slightest doubt that the average boy and girl in school or college does not look with favour on a career of mere selfish acquisition.

Many of them will read with respect a book that tells them that religion is a base superstition; they will listen calmly to a speaker who is a professional atheist. But if a teacher or an orator should tell them that altruism is ridiculous, that what they ought to do is to get all they can for themselves and not bother about public service, they would laugh at him—at any rate they would not take him seriously. Even the most ambitious young men and women feel some degree of responsibility to their community and to the world; they hope not only to be successful, they hope to be useful. They do not loudly articulate these ideals, but they have them. When I hear unduly anxious middle-aged college alumni deplore the "loose morals" of youth, my hope is that when these boys and girls reach the age of forty-five they will have as fine ideals as they have now.

And was there ever a period of human history when social service and social responsibility were more exciting than now? Social problems have become a real drama, more exciting than any representation in metropolitan theatres. For the very foundations of Economics are challenged. When we consider the conditions in Russia and in Italy and in Spain; when we see a nation so normally stable as Germany losing equilibrium; the study of Economics and Sociology has become wildly exciting.

[III]

TEACHING STUDENTS TO STUDY

"UNIVERSITIES—American, English, German," by Abraham Flexner, is a book that should be read by intelligent Americans, especially those professionally associated with colleges and universities; it will hurt their feelings but not their minds. Our schools, all our institutions, need adverse criticism, and perhaps the more severe it is, the more profitable it may be. And it is a book that I wish no foreigner would read; many foreigners believe our business men are all Babbitts and our small towns all Main Streets. Mr. Flexner will make most of them believe that our representative American universities are chiefly engaged in the promulgation of the cheapest form of vulgarities. Every man who hates America will love this book.

39

There are two ways in which one may meet a reproof, an insult, a misrepresentation, a caricature. The victim may fly into a rage, hotly deny every accusation, hurl insults back at their source, OR—however unpalatable the indictment may be, he can give it thoughtful and dispassionate consideration, asking himself why the attack was made, and trying to see if there is not some ground for it. Rage and resentment lead to nothing good; honest heart-searching may turn an accusation into a means of grace.

American universities, in their endeavour to be of "service," have gone to such lengths of specific instruction in various details, some of which bear no relation to learning or scholarship, that they are—every one of them—in danger of forgetting the particular thing which should be their distinction. Universities, like monasteries, are in the world but they should not be of the world. They serve an ideal which the world never has understood and can never understand—*pure learning,* without regard to its practical value. So far as teaching students is concerned, the main purpose should be the enrichment, the strengthening, the development, the elevation of the mind by serious studies, rather than the crowding of the mind by information, or showing students how to "do things" which any educated man can learn for and by himself. Education and not instruction is the true aim; and in this most American professors will agree with Mr. Flexner, and will be glad that he has put particular emphasis where it belongs.

The President of a University should be a scholar rather than a business man; because it is easier for a scholar to master the details of academic business management than it is for a business man to master academic scholarship.

This does not mean that I believe scholars to be superior to business men; all I mean is they have a different kind of work, that must be learned in a different way. It is easy enough for sheltered academic scholars to sneer at those who provide the shelter. No university, no matter how austere its aim, could exist five minutes without the aid of business men. For clergymen do not build churches; physicians do not build hospitals; research scholars in chemistry do not build laboratories; professors do not build libraries or class-rooms. These edifices and tools are provided by business men who believe in professional men without wishing to imitate them.

In all schools and colleges, the most exciting problem of administrative officers is precisely that which confronts the staff of teachers: *What shall we do to make the students want to study?* To a visitor from another planet who knew

41

nothing about either schools or human nature, the question would seem to savour of absurdity. It would seem like asking: What shall we do to make fish swim, or birds fly? For surely the word student means one who studies; surely schools and universities, founded for the one purpose of encouraging learning, must be centres of intellectual life. But the facts are otherwise.

The facts are, of course, that the normal, healthy boy or girl never naturally took to learning; and the modern school or university is filled with powerful influences that militate against the intellectual life. Just as the spiritual atmosphere of the world outside is so unhealthy that only robust and determined men and women are able to fight it sufficiently to work out their own salvation, so the boy or girl in college who really wishes to live the life of the mind finds that the intellectual climate is unfavourable. Indeed I think there is only one department of the modern university where there can truly be said to exist an intellectual atmosphere. This is the Graduate School.

The Law School, the Medical School, and other professional schools are filled with students who study with chronic ardour, but the reason for this is that they see a direct connexion between the course of study and their bread and butter. Commercial rather than intellectual ambition is the driving force.

In the average secondary school and college of liberal arts, the athletic and social extra-curriculum activities exert a tremendous pulling force not only away from the curriculum, but from the intellectual life. And these influences, like bodily temptations, have a formidable ally in natural instincts. Just as it is natural for an average youth to prefer outdoor games to indoor study, so it is natural for an average youth to prefer the rewards given him by his classmates to those bestowed on him by his teachers. The modern school and college is no place for the loafer; indeed I think if there were more idlers the situation might be improved. It is a hotbed of activity. There are boys and girls who work harder and more continuously in school and college than they will ever work in later life; but their work has nothing to do with the course of study. Trying to "make" the various athletic teams—and the present excitement over hockey, basketball, swimming, boxing, wrestling, fencing, indoor track meets leaves no period from September to July quiescent. One of the numerous paradoxes is that swimming is a winter sport.

Then the competition for a place on the college or school journals—something difficult to explain to a foreigner—the constant dances, the week-end excursion to woman's colleges or to a neighbouring large city, the competition for Manager and Assistant Manager of the innumerable athletic teams, the passionate desire to "make" a secret society, with all the time given to "holdouts," initiations, banquets, etc., leave the average student little room for mental work.

At practically all colleges, dancing has become a major sport. It is said that if the visiting preacher, carefully selected for his reputation as a Sunday church-filler in his home town, wishes to preach to the students of Harvard, Yale, Princeton on a Sunday, he should preach at Vassar, Wellesley, Bryn Mawr, or Smith.

Football, which used to be an athletic event, is now a social event. The game of the year means two hours of football sandwiched in among forty-eight hours of dancing.

The average student is a busy man—there is no chance for idleness—his only economies are in sleep and in the purchase of textbooks.

Sometimes I think the happiest man in college is the so-called "grind," who, curiously enough, is not nearly so greatly despised as he used to be. The fact is that he is not only enviable, he is envied. To a student trying to win a place on the daily paper, or on an athletic team, or in a secret society, the spectacle of a classmate who has nothing to do but study—who has no imperious engagements caused by ruthless competition, who can actually go to the University Library for a quiet hour of reading—is often appealing. I remember one Yale undergraduate, an attractive and clever youth, who had been popular and "prominent" all through the four years of college, telling me sadly that he wished he might return for one year in the Graduate School, not to become a teacher, but merely to have the privilege of undisturbed study. "I wanted to study while in college, but during the whole four years I never had one single hour when I was not interrupted."

Thus every modern American institution of learning is a beehive of non-intellectual activities.

Faculty meetings, committee meetings of administrative officers, are frequently devoted to the problem of trying to combat these allurements.

But even if there were no outside extra-curriculum centrifugal forces, there would still be the age-old problem, What shall we do to make the students want to study?

We know well enough that in Elizabethan England Oxford and Cambridge were not, so far as the undergraduates were concerned, centres of intellectual activity. The University Wits were more famous for dissipation than for

45

scholarship. In the eighteenth century, the amount of drinking done every week in the universities would make the twentieth century student seem like an ascetic.

Reading the *Confessions of an Oxford Don*, published in the nineteenth century, I was impressed by the fact that he had exactly the same problems that confront a modern American college Dean—how could he induce the students to study? The number of undergraduates who had imperative and frequent dentist appointments in London; those whose distant relatives gave frequent evidence of mortality; those whose health permitted them to do everything except their work. These things seem to suggest that the more things change the more they remain the same.

Thus I have myself little faith in new systems, in new methods, in schemes of reform; as the eternal problem is human nature, it would appear that the best way to deal with eternal youth is not by a new system, for even a perfect system depends for its success on imperfect human administration; but rather by obtaining wherever it is possible, both in school and in college, the best *teachers*—that is to say, teachers who know both the subject and the object—who know their speciality and who understand the nature of youth.

Every university must have first-class scholars, men whose work in research is of such a quality that they command the respect of their peers in Europe and in America. Such men, when their productive work is really of the highest grade (not merely of local reputation) are the glory of a university and the flower of scholarship. Some of these men combine excellence in teaching with genius in research; and in a Graduate School, it does not matter whether they can teach well or not, their very reputation will inspire their pupils—even as in the field of morals and religion a good life is more powerful in its influence than rhetorical display.

And a "good teacher" who does not grow intellectually will soon or later cease to be a good teacher. But teaching is an art, not a science; and a first-rate teacher whose main productive work is not in the printed page, but in the minds and characters of his pupils, is surely a valuable man in any school and college, and a useful man in any community.

In the teaching of students to study, I should either directly or indirectly encourage excitement. Not every assiduous student has the terrific passion of Browning's Grammarian; not every plodder has the chronic zeal of Faust's famulus, Wagner, "who, when he finds an angleworm, rejoices!"

47

But there are many idle and indifferent under-graduates who know they are missing something as they loaf along. There are times when they envy the students who study because they want to study. And surely excitement is the right word to describe the emotion of those who are making laboratory experiments by themselves; those who are specialising in a given period of political history; and those who are studying contemporary movements in the theatre, or social developments in Europe.

[IV]

THE EXCITING QUEST FOR IDEALS

NO MATTER how many false prophets
have gone out into the world, no matter
if some of them are in University faculties, no
matter if every fundamental principle not only
in religion, but in morals and what seems to some
persons even more important, in economics, is
publicly challenged, there is no doubt in my
mind that schools and colleges are now, even
more than ever, the homes of idealism. And this
idealism shows itself particularly where there is
freedom of thought and liberty of expression.
The ideal of service does not necessarily mean
an enforced and standardised patriotism. I believe the best patriots are those who have the
courage and the brains to think for themselves
and to declare their opinions, even though those
opinions may run counter to received community

49

sentiment. No university is worthy of the name, that does not, with all its discipline and culture, encourage its students to think for themselves. Let them in later years sacrifice their money for the public good; but they should not sacrifice their convictions for anything.

I am glad to see this matter expressed with his customary felicity by Sir James Barrie, in his address called *The Entrancing Life*, delivered on his installation as Chancellor of Edinburgh University in 1930, and now available in print. Here is an extract where he discusses the aim of Scottish universities: the "needs of the genius of the Scottish people."

Those needs are that every child born into this country shall as far as possible have an equal chance. The words "as far as possible" tarnish the splendid hope, and they were not in the original dream. Some day we may be able to cast them out. It is by Education, though not merely in the smaller commoner meaning of the word, that the chance is to be got. Since the war various nations have wakened to its being the one way out; they know its value so well that perhaps the only safe boast left to us is that we knew it first. They seem, however, to be setting about the work with ultimate objects that are not ours. Their student from his earliest age is being brought up to absorb the ideas of his political rulers. That is the all of his education, not merely in his academic studies but in all his social life, all his mind, all his relaxations; they are in control from his birth, and he is to emerge into citizenship with rigid convictions which it is trusted will last his lifetime. The systems vary in different lands, but that seems to be their trend, and I tell you they are being carried out with thoroughness. Nothing can depart more from the Scottish idea, which I take to be to educate our men and women primarily not for their country's good but for their own, not so much to teach them what to think as how to think, not preparing them to give as little trouble as possible in the future but sending them into it in the hope that they will give trouble.

And the eternal idealism which should be characteristic of youth in primary schools, secondary schools, and universities, is approved by Sir James Barrie in this paragraph from the same address:

Is it Lochaber no more for you? I don't believe it. The flavour cannot have gone out of the peat. The haggis can still charge uphill. I'll tell you a secret. Have you an unwonted delicious feeling on the tops of your heads at this moment, as if an angel's wing had brushed them half an hour or so ago? It did—I speak from memory; and it carried with it a message from your University: "All hopelessness abandon, ye who have entered here." She trusts your wallets contain, as her parting gift to you, "those instruments with which high spirits call the future from its cradle."

Even in the most sophisticated American colleges, like Harvard, Princeton, Yale, Columbia,

I believe that romanticism is still rampant. The undergraduates understand Hotspur more readily than they understand Falstaff; especially when these two respectively reflect on the meaning of the word *honour*.

And many students, who in their Sophomore year pass through that particular Slough of Despond called Irony, regain their hope and their faith before graduation. Browning was an optimist; yet he suffered in adolescence from the contagious disease Keats so perfectly described in his preface to *Endymion*.

The imagination of a boy is healthy, and the mature imagination of a man is healthy; but there is a space of life between, in which the soul is in a ferment, the character undecided, the way of life uncertain, the ambition thick-sighted: thence proceeds mawkishness, and all the thousand bitters which those men I speak of must necessarily taste in going over the following pages.

If we did not have Browning's first poem, *Pauline,* which he tried in vain to suppress, we should have no evidence that he had passed through his *Sturm und Drang*. In *Pauline,* which he produced at the age of twenty, we see that he lived for a time in that intellectual bog where the mind reacts on itself, where mockery takes the place of enthusiasm, where irony usurps the throne of faith, where cynicism supplants hope.

> First went my hopes of perfecting mankind,
> Next, faith in them, and faith in Freedom's self
> And Virtue's self, then my own motives, ends
> And aims and loves, and human love went last.
> I felt this no decay, because new powers,
> Rose as old feelings left—wit, mockery,
> Light-heartedness; for I had oft been sad,
> Mistrusting my resolves, but now I cast
> Hope joyously away;

That is to say, Browning, like many adolescent men and women, felt that in substituting wit, mockery, irony, for enthusiasm, faith, hope, he had made an intellectual advance; he had matured. He regarded this change with complacency, for there is no conceit and self-satisfaction, no awareness of intellectual superiority like that of the sophisticated. But, like many undergraduates, he made a complete recovery, which was proved by the return of romanticism. He was like one, who, having lost the faith of a child, finally, after many difficulties, replaces it by the faith of a man.

In every period of academic history, a certain number of original and independent undergraduates have rebelled both against the curriculum and against the atmosphere of the University. We know that in the middle of the eighteenth century, Thomas Gray ridiculed the curriculum and the faculty at Cambridge; and later a bitter cry came from the heart of William Wordsworth when he was an undergraduate at the same University. I quote from the *Prelude:*

And here was Labour, his own bond-slave; Hope,
That never set the pains against the prize;
Idleness halting with his weary clog,
And poor misguided Shame, and witless Fear,
And simple Pleasure foraging for Death;
Honour misplaced, and Dignity astray;
Feuds, factions, flatteries, enmity, and guile
Murmuring submission, and bald government,
(The idol weak as the idolator),
And Decency and Custom starving Truth,
And blind Authority beating with his staff
The child that might have led him; Emptiness
Followed as of good omen, and meek Worth
Left to herself unheard of and unknown.

And here is a suppressed sonnet by Tennyson:

SONNET ON CAMBRIDGE UNIVERSITY

Therefore your Halls, your ancient Colleges,
Your portals statued with old kings and queens,
Your gardens, myriad-volumed libraries,
Wax-lighted chapels, and rich carven screens,
Your doctors, and your proctors, and your deans
Shall not avail you, when the Day-beam sports
New-risen o'er awaken'd Albion—No!

54

Nor yet your solemn organ-pipes that blow
Melodious thunders thro' your vacant courts
At morn and eve—because your manner sorts
Not with this age wherefrom ye stand apart—
Because the lips of little children preach
Against you, you that do profess to teach
And teach us nothing, feeding not the heart.

The transition from boarding school to the university is nothing like so dramatic as that from High School. The boy who has left home for a famous prep school at the age of eleven or twelve, and then entered the university at the age of eighteen, has discounted the insulation and excitement of college life. But the boy who has never been away from home, who has attended a High School or a Day School in his native town, where every night has been spent with his parents, he, on entering a University as a Freshman, undergoes a transformation. It is a new and exciting adventure.

I was a High School Boy, and although I loved my father and mother, and my life at home was happy, I naturally, with the ardour of youth for almost anything new and strange, looked forward to entering college with indescribable eagerness. When I was sixteen or seventeen, I used to go to New Haven on a Saturday to see some big football game; and although the football players seemed to me mythical heroes, it was neither the players nor the contest that gave me the spinal thrill. It was the sight of the undergraduates returning from the arena.

When the game was over, there being in those days no automobiles or trolley cars, the majority of students walked from the scene of battle to their lodgings. In the November twilight, I mingled with this throng; and when we reached the entrance to the Campus on Chapel Street, then came the separation. They entered the gates of Paradise, while I had to continue down Chapel Street to the railway station, and take the train.

I used to stand still and watch them carelessly entering that sacred enclosure; and even if some day I see the blessed angels entering into the City of Gold, I shall not feel any greater longing than I felt then. To think that those fortunate youths lived in dormitories! That they ate together, went to classes together, played games together, had their work and their recreation in common!

Well, I have always been one of those fortunate persons who are not easily disillusioned; when I came myself to this Academic Paradise, and had a dormitory room on the top floor of North Middle, I felt no puncture of my iridescent dreams. It was wonderful to go to chapel in the morning, see the tremendous Seniors take their places, and feel that I too was a part of this tradition—I too belonged to this community fellowship. It was exciting to go to classes on Saturdays, something I had never done before. Exciting to go to a class at five in the afternoon, as strange in my experience as if it were five in the morning. To eat at a club of my fellows instead of at home. These delights had a savour all their own.

Only I found that the real mark of the sophisticated undergraduate was not to show too much enthusiasm; in other words, adolescence, in so many aspects the unhappiest years of a man's life, had set in, and established a pagan worship of false gods. In this valley of the shadow of death, I regret to say that I was encouraged not only by many classmates, but by some members of the Faculty; who themselves seemed to regard anything like intellectual enthusiasm as men of the world regard the naïve raptures of the unsophisticated. Such men did me no good; but fortunately I escaped eventually from their sterilising influences.

Between January and April many Freshmen and even many Sophomores suffer terribly, although outwardly they may put up a good façade. There is no Confessional to relieve their minds; there are no outdoor sports at that

57

time of the year to relieve their bodies; their early enthusiasms have given place to routine, or they have been flattened by the irony of their mates or the more destructive irony of their elders.

Here is where the right kind of teaching and the right kind of teachers have their opportunity; here is the golden chance to awaken a thirst for the pleasures of the mind, for the development of the intellectual life, yes, for the birth of the soul. The excitement of teaching, the knowledge that something greater than mere acquisition of facts is at stake, reaches its climax.

And I believe that every undergraduate, however sophisticated he may wish to appear, is at heart an incurable romantic. The appeal to idealism through the teaching of great literature, will awaken some response.

"Certain bells, now mute, can jingle."

For what does the loss of ideals mean? It means the loss of excitement. Ideals give significance to life. When a man has completely lost his ideals, he has lost interest. Not only his daily life becomes meaningless but Life itself, has, with the loss of its meaning, lost also its savour. "I am content to die," said Renan, "but I should like to know whether death will be of any use to me."

One of the most important results of a school or college education should be increased zest for living. But this cannot come through mere accomplishments; it comes through a passion for life, that is, through excitement. Browning, in his poem, *The Statue and the Bust,* describes a brilliant, accomplished, purposeless young aristocrat as a *sheath without a sword.* A sheath may be adorned outwardly with beautiful works of art; but a sheath is meant to hold a sword and it is as ridiculous without a sword as a ship on dry land. The privilege of the teacher is to put a sword into that sheath; to give not merely energy, but purpose; so that the students, properly armed, will go forth on the exciting adventure of life—a knightly loyalty to commanding ideals.

[V]

NOBLE RAGE REPRESSED BY PENURY

IT IS both strange and unfortunate that the particular group of men and women who are perhaps of more value to the United States of America than any other class, should on the whole be the poorest paid. The teachers in primary and secondary schools have the future of our country in their hands; they take the raw material—for there is nothing more nearly raw than a child—and fashion it into citizenship.

The prodigious advance on the material side of school-teaching has by no means been accompanied by an improved status for the teacher. A foreigner visiting America for the first time would see many things to excite his wonder; let us hope both his wonder and his admiration; but anyhow his wonder. And perhaps of all the material glories of our country, the thing that would astonish him most would be the edifices and equipment of our public schools.

He would see everywhere primary and secondary school buildings imposing and magnificent; with schoolrooms well lighted, well ventilated, and adorned with the treasures of art; he would see remarkably complete gymnasiums and playing fields and often swimming pools. He would discover that the eyes, the teeth, and the general health of the children are cared for *gratis* by experienced specialists; he would see that the text-books are free, so that every child has the advantages of a palatial building, good light, good air, every opportunity for sport, with free books and free medical attendance.

The only thing he would not be sure of is that the boys and girls are being educated. Listen to Socrates:

If you were going to commit your body to someone, who might do good or harm to it, would you not carefully consider and ask the opinion of your friends and kindred, and deliberate many days as to whether you should give him the care of your body? But when the soul is in question, which you hold to be of far more value than the body, and upon the good or evil of which depends the well-being of your all;—about this you never consulted either with your father or your mother or with your brother or with any one of us who are your companions. . . . For there is far greater peril in buying knowledge than in buying meat and drink: the one you purchase of the wholesale or retail dealer, and carry them away in other vessels, and before you receive them into the body as food, you may deposit them at home and call in any experienced friend who knows what is good to be eaten or drunken, and what not, and how much, and when; and then the danger of purchasing them is not so great. But you cannot buy the wares of knowledge and carry them away in another vessel; when you have paid for them you must receive them into the soul and go your way, either greatly harmed or greatly benefited.

President Eliot of Harvard was scandalised because the coach of the football team received a larger salary than any professor on the faculty; but as a matter of fact, this business simply followed the law of supply and demand. Research scholars are more numerous than first-class football coaches; and the football coach is in many instances the ablest *teacher* connected with the "institution of learning." If the poor quality of teaching, common enough in college faculties, was displayed by the football coach, he would lose his job; furthermore if he does not produce victory fairly often, he will lose his job. What would happen to college teachers if their tenure of appointment were determined by the scholarly efficiency of their pupils?

The law of supply and demand does not apply

so rigidly to teachers and preachers as it does to lawyers and merchants; because there are plenty of preachers and teachers who enter their profession actuated mainly by unselfish ideals. But unhappily or not, the law does apply fairly accurately; in a tiny village church, where the salary is small, the pastor is usually not a man of brilliant intellectual gifts or of persuasive eloquence; whereas in a New York or Chicago church, you usually find an able minister. People reach their levels here as elsewhere.

Thus the way to get better teachers in the public schools is to pay more salary. After we have spent vast sums on buildings, apparatus, and a'hletic fields, we might spend a little more on teaching.

There are nearly one million teachers in America. Yet no profession is so almost forgotten by the public. There is nothing spectacular about teachers; the only way a schoolteacher can attract public attention is by doing something scandalous, giving a pupil cruel or unusual punishment, being suspected of disloyalty to the flag, sexual irregularity, saying something sensational.

To some parents any penalty imposed on their child seems cruel. There is a difference here between America and Germany. In Germany if a boy gets a whipping at school, he gets another

63

when he reaches home. In America, if a boy gets a whipping at school, his father goes to the school and tries to whip the teacher.

Money spent on education in America is a good investment; men and women who are educated are comparatively free from superstition, have the power of initiative, will think and act for themselves. The supreme obstacle to Communism and other political and economic fallacies in America is the High School. It seems to me evident that the reason Russia submitted for centuries—and long after it became an anachronism—to a capricious, irresponsible, absolute government by the Tsars, was that so many of the people were illiterate. And the reason now why a Committee of Communists, backed by the army and the secret police, can hold the whole country under a Soviet domination, is that so many of the people are illiterate. The reason why their State religion under the Tsars was a mass of superstitions was the illiteracy of the people; and the reason why the National religion is now Atheism is the illiteracy of the people.

Teachers must receive enough salary to be able to devote their chief energy to teaching. "Where your treasure is, there will your heart be also." But if there is no treasure there will be no heart.

Aristotle said, "Those who teach children well

are more to be honored than even their parents, for these only give them life, those the art of living well."

Yet, although teachers are under-paid and many of them under-nourished, although their nerves are shaken every day, they are for the most part a *happy* group of people, happier than almost any other group except ministers of the gospel, nuns, and priests. We use the common phrase, "happy as a boy let out of school." But it lacks the significance of "happy as a teacher let out of school." Teachers on a vacation, travelling, or in a convention, are a cheerful crowd. And they have a greater advantage over their pupils, for many are happy even *in* school.

I remember addressing every day for six days at San Antonio, Texas, a convention of public-school teachers. It was early in September. The thermometer registered over one hundred degrees every day, and the teachers were about to begin the "long grind" of the academic year. They were such a cheerful, high-hearted set of men and women that it was a delight to talk to them. In California, in New York City and other places where summer schools are directed by the universities, a large number of the students are public-school teachers, taking a "bus-man's holiday." The average teacher enjoys teaching and enjoys learning. In the immortal words of Chaucer describing the Oxford scholar

"And gladly wolde he lerne, and gladly teche."

They have found the secret of happiness in congenial work with an unselfish aim.

Teaching any subject is the best way to learn it. Teaching disciplines the mind of the teacher; it is essential for him to make his meaning clear. Thus school-teaching is an admirable preparation for law or medicine or politics or bondselling, in fact, for almost anything. Yet there is a reasonable doubt whether those who take up teaching as a makeshift or a springboard or a stepping-stone or for immediate though scanty emolument, are in general a brilliant ornament to the profession. I well remember years ago, Mr. James McConaughy, the father of the present President of Wesleyan University, presiding at a public meeting where a speaker, addressing an audience of young men, advised them to teach for a couple of years after graduation from college: "It will be a good thing for you!" Mr. McConaughy interrupted by saying, "It will possibly be better for you than for the school."

On the other hand, I remember a surprising letter I had from one of the most inspiring Headmasters in America, the late Doctor Warren of Albany Academy. He wrote asking if I could recommend a young man for teaching in his school. I replied that I could recommend an admirable candidate, only I must modify the recommendation by the fact that he had no intention of remaining as a teacher in Albany or of following the teaching profession. To my surprise Doctor Warren wrote: "He is just the man I want! The fact that he is using this job as a makeshift shows he has brains!" Make out of that what you can.

Many men and women, when they think of the teacher at all, imagine that teaching must be a dull affair. On the contrary, teaching is wildly exciting, adventurous, romantic, with no two days alike. The successful teacher loves what he teaches and whom he teaches. In the schoolroom, he is in absolute command, although in one sense he is as lonely as a captain on a battleship. He may receive good advice from his Principal and his colleagues; but when he enters his classroom, shuts the door, and looks into the faces of the boys and girls, no one can help him except himself. His teaching and his discipline depend solely on his mind and personality. This is a tragedy if he is incompetent; but what splendid excitement if he is equal to the situation!

Teaching is an art, not a science; it is one of the greatest of all the arts; and after teaching steadily for forty years and enjoying it, I feel that I know little about it. The first necessity of the teacher as soon as he takes his place at the desk, is to arouse the interest of his pupils. They do not come into the room eager to learn or with their minds on the subject. They are thinking of what they have just been doing or of what they are going to do as soon as they are released. He must turn their minds from all these other interests and recreations and persuade them to follow the lesson as a hunting dog follows the scent.

But not only do the *pupils* come into the room thinking of something else; only too often does this apply with even greater emphasis to the teacher. He has just been doing some original work; his wife had a baby last night; he wonders how he is going to pay the coal bill; a distant relative has suddenly arrived for a visit; there are many worries and household and personal problems in his mind. Everyone of these must be swept out, and he must give himself wholly to the matter in hand.

And right here is one reason for the happiness and value of teaching. He MUST give himself to the matter in hand. The grocer's clerk and the bank clerk, anyone engaged in routine, mechanical, or manual labour, can do his work while still thinking of his personal griefs and worries; but the teacher cannot. He cannot teach while thinking of anything else. This is fortunate.

Although Dorothy Canfield does not say so, it appeared to me an evident truth while reading the novel, *Her Son's Wife*. Her heroine is a mother who was a professional school-teacher; she had such horrible worry and trouble at home that it might almost be called chronically acute. The crisis lasted not for days but for several years; every moment at home was hell, and she could neither eat nor sleep with any satisfaction. All these years she was an active and successful school-teacher. The unthinking reader might wonder why she did not break down. How could she with those corroding anxieties, do her work? *But it was the work that kept her from breaking down.* There is an immense histrionic element in teaching. Just as the actor, though filled with grief and anxiety, must amuse his audience every night, so the teacher must play his part; and a very good thing it is for both.

Speaking only for myself, I will say honestly that with me teaching is more than an art or an occupation. It is a passion. I love to teach as a painter loves to paint, as a singer loves to sing, as a poet loves to write. Before I get out of bed in the morning, I think with ardent delight of my first group of students.

I almost laugh aloud when I remember what

a business man said to me more than forty years ago. I told him I expected to become a teacher: "Oh, that's terrible. You will enjoy the novelty of it for perhaps two or three years. Then you will get into a rut, become a drudge, and you will be cut off from the exciting life of the world." Prophecies are usually inaccurate; it is the way of prophecies; but I can think of none more ludicrously false than this.

The chief happiness of the teacher is in the influence he exerts on the minds of his pupils, and of the intimate, permanent friendships that result. It is truly a great profession, one of the most mentally and spiritually rewarding in the whole world. And the teacher's personality is remembered by his pupils all their lives, sometimes with contempt, sometimes with anger, sometimes with amusement—and sometimes with profound respect and gratitude.

In the High School at Hartford, I had a teacher, Doctor W. R. Martin, now within the last mystery. He had an unquenchable thirst for learning; a raging passion for knowledge and ideas, which somehow touched and illuminated our dull, stupid, immature minds. Never shall I forget that man.

And there were also other teachers whose influence in my life is as elevating as it is permanent. There is no limit to the range of a good word, well spoken at the right time.

I believe there are some teachers who really teach life. I can remember one or two. They taught it by precept, they taught it by example. Isn't this very thing—how to live one's daily life—what most young people today are searching for?

It is indeed; and if they are to be guided, assisted, or inspired in this search, the teacher must have a mind sufficiently free from sordid cares. I shall never forget what one teacher told me. "You may think I am interested in my pupils, but I am not. You may think I am interested in research work, but I am not. The only thing in which I take any interest is whether or not I can pay my bills. This question has driven everything else out of my mind." A few months later, he committed suicide.

[VI]

STRANGE OPTIMISM OF THE POLICEMEN

ONE OF the excitements of teaching in the twentieth century comes from the fact that never before in history was there such universal eagerness for an education. The teacher sells a commodity in universal demand. Such a situation has the defects of its qualities; hundreds of boys and girls are "sent" to college who would be better off elsewhere. But more desirable is such a condition than a general lack of education, or what would be even worse, a lack of desire for it. It would be a tragedy for individuals and for the community. Carlyle said, "That one soul should remain in ignorance who was capable of knowledge, that I call a tragedy." Better have fifty incapable students in college than one capable man left out.

And what after all is the general average of

the character of school-boys and school-girls, of college youth, of the younger generation? Well, it is a significant fact that most school principals and most college Deans are optimists.

The Headmaster of a private school and Principal of a public school and the Dean of a College see the worst side of student life. Among the vast number of books on the subject, I recommend that fathers and mothers, and all others who are interested, read the various books on college life written by Dean Briggs of Harvard; and *The Boy Today* by Doctor Mather Abbott of Lawrenceville School; and *Life at College* by Dean Christian Gauss of Princeton. I have known intimately three Deans of Yale College—Henry P. Wright, Frederick S. Jones, and Clarence W. Mendell, who adorns that office today. Such men come into intimate contact with the seamy side of school and college life; and as by the necessity of their profession they see more of the undesirable students than of the steady workers, it would not be surprising if these college officers were pessimistic not only on the condition of undergraduate life, but on the younger generation in general.

The contrary is the case. These men, psychological experts, academic policemen, *believe in modern youth*. Mr. Mendell says that if a student should come to college to study human nature, he might learn most about the subject by sitting in the Dean's office for a week.

A sense of humour, characteristic of these men I have mentioned, helps them in their work, and helps to keep them interested. For the resources of some lazy or indifferent students are amazing. If these original youths spent half the time and energy in doing an assigned task that they spend in avoiding it, they might attain to high honours.

The originality of lazy undergraduates is often startling. I remember a man in my class at Yale, who received what was meant to be a final summons to the office of Dean Wright. The Dean told him that he had so many overcuts and excess of absences from classroom and chapel, that all would be cancelled, but only on one condition. "Tomorrow," said the Dean solemnly, "you begin with a clean slate. But you understand no excuses will be accepted. You cannot have any more illnesses, for you have already had all those that are known in the history of medicine. There cannot possibly be any more deaths in your family, for every one of your relatives has died, and several have died more than once." The boy thanked him and withdrew; the next morning he cut chapel, and sent in as an excuse that he had suffered from a sudden and acute attack of *"agoraphobia."* The Dean was so amused that he excused him.

I asked my classmate how in the world he happened to think of that. "Well," he replied "I had had all the familiar ills that flesh is heir to. I therefore opened Webster's Unabridged Dictionary, to see if I could not find some new and convincing disease. Imagine my delight on finding, at almost the first crack out of the box *agoraphobia,* a fear of large open spaces, and how perfectly it applied to chapel!"

Another undergraduate of charming manners who, so far as I could discover, did no work went through college and got his degree even as some persons who never pay their bills or meet their obligations, go successfully through life. He met every emergency with a grace of humour so unexpected as to be irresistible. One day a professor of Greek, conducting a recitation where nobody seemed to know anything, lost his temper, and exclaimed petulantly, "There are only three men in this class who do not use translations!" This particular scapegrace immediately enquired "Who are the other two, Professor?"

There is a good deal of drudgery in teaching, though not more than in other professions or occupations; and the chief drudgery is reading examination papers. Yet even this desert has its oases of humour. Years ago I put on an examination paper a question about the life of Browning. One answer was, "Browning died in 1889. In that same year I was born. What a fearful exchange!" And we sometimes learn by the answer what *not* to ask. On a Tennyson paper I set the question, "What ultimately became of Dora?" A youth wrote, "She died." And on an examination in ancient history, the professor asked, "Can you give the date of the battle of Munda?" The youth replied, "I can." On a Chaucer examination, I asked the students to draw a map of the road from London to Canterbury, marking the places where the pilgrims rested on the way. One young man made an elaborate map, pointing out accurately every spot. Then he erected signs along the highway —BOVRIL, USE BEECHAM'S PILLS, PIONEER TOBACCO, showing he was a realist as well as a historian.

[VII]

THE MOST THRILLING OF PROFESSIONS

EVERYBODY knows or ought to know that in every school and college there is a great loss of time and efficiency, if one judges the success of courses by the practical knowledge gained by the pupils. Browning, who was educated by private tutors, and who therefore at the age of twenty had more actual knowledge than any university graduate, used to express regret that he had never had the advantages of Oxford or Cambridge. And he could not understand how it was possible for men to graduate from a university and know so little; though any university man could have told him. In a large class of students, not very much definite knowledge of the subject is gained by the individuals. It is certain that with a private tutor, one would learn to read or speak a foreign language more efficiently and in less time than in any college course.

Suppose a teacher of the piano had a class of forty pupils and called on each one to go to the piano in the room and work at it for five minutes, which would mean that each one would play perhaps once in three weeks. Such pupils might attend such a class for three hundred years and not be able to play a piece of music.

Thus for actual efficiency the private tutor with one pupil, or with a very small class is the only method; for this reason at West Point and at Annapolis and at some colleges the classes are restricted to about seven students; efficiency is the aim.

Yet in a fairly large division, with the ordinary method of lecture or recitation, there is an excitement both in teaching and in being taught, that can hardly be the case with one or with seven pupils. The spirit of competition, the necessity of keeping the whole class interested, the dramatic quality of the scene, have elements that may produce more stimulation and more excitement than could be attained by a result more definite.

In the six preceding sections, I have endeavoured to set forth Literature as a Revelation of Life, and therefore of transcendent importance: to indicate, in accordance with the noble traditions of English Public Schools, the Five Pillars of Education; the rare and difficult Art of Teaching Students to Study: the Romantic Excitement of the Modern Quest for Ideals: the Chilling and Crippling Effects of Expensive Penury: the Unexpected and Strange Optimism of Academic Policemen.

The observations made in these six chapters came not from a hopeful imagination but from actual experience.

So far from being a dull routine, teaching is to me the most adventurous, the most exciting, the most thrilling of professions. It has its perils, its discouragements, its successes, its delights. Browning says,

"It's an awkward thing to play with souls," and whenever I enter a classroom filled with young men, I think of them not as a class or as a group; but as a collection of individual personalities more complex, more delicate, more intricate than any machinery. Not only is every student an organism more sensitive than any mechanical product, every student is infinitely precious to some parent or to some relative who may be three thousand miles away. That is why the teacher should never use irony or sarcasm or the language that humiliates; that is why he should never take the attitude of suspicion or depreciation. The officials at the United States

79

Mint, the Head of a diamond mine, the President of a metropolitan bank are not dealing with material so valuable as that in the hands of the teacher. Their mistakes are not so disastrous as his; their success is not so important.

The excitement of teaching comes from the fact that one is teaching a subject one loves to individuals who are worth more than all the money in the world.

THE END